COMING TO REST

Coming to Rest

POEMS

KATHRYN STRIPLING BYER

LOUISIANA STATE UNIVERSITY PRESS))((BATON ROUGE

Published by Louisiana State University Press

Copyright © 2006 by Kathryn Stripling Byer

All rights reserved

Manufactured in the United States of America

First printing

DESIGNER: AMANDA MCDONALD SCALLAN

TYPEFACE: MINION, WITH ZAPFINO DISPLAY

PRINTER AND BINDER: EDWARDS BROTHERS, INC.

Library of Congress Cataloging-in-Publication Data

Byer, Kathryn Stripling.

  Coming to rest : poems / Kathryn Stripling Byer.

    p. cm.

  Includes bibliographical references.

  ISBN 0-8071-3134-2 (cloth : alk. paper) — ISBN 0-8071-3135-0 (pbk. : alk. paper)

  I. Title.

PS3569.T6965C66 2006

811'.54—dc22

2005018515

Grateful acknowledgment is made to the editors of the following publications, in which the poems noted first appeared: *ALCA-Lines:* "Cumberland Gap"; *The Atlantic Monthly:* "Her Daughter"; *The Blue Moon Review:* "Closer"; *Carolina Quarterly:* "Still Life" (as "Stilleben"); *The Cortland Review:* "Coming to Rest" (as "Coming to Rest, Again"); *Emrys Journal:* "Halloween"; *The Greensboro Review (Special Issue: A Tribute to Robert Watson):* "The Exotics"; *Iron Mountain Review:* "Scuppernongs"; *Shenandoah:* "Coastal Plain" and "Still to Us at Twilight"; *Southern Poetry Review:* "Black Road" and "Hallows" (as "Three Dawns"); *Now and Then:* "Tent Dream"; *Southern Review:* "Pneumonia"; *Victoria Press:* "Halloween Again" (in a much different version); *Mint Museum of Charlotte, Special Edition of Art and Writing by NC Arts Fellowship Winners, 1988:* "Nets"; *storySouth:* "Chicago Bound," "Halloween Again," and "The Still Here and Now."

  "I Listen" appeared first as "Listen," in *Catching Light* (LSU Press, 2002).

  "Self-Portrait with Shades," from *Wake*, a chapbook, Spring Street Editions, 2003.

  Excerpt from "The Birthplace" from *Opened Ground: Selected Poems 1966–1996* by Seamus Heaney. Copyright © 1998 by Seamus Heaney. Reprinted by permission of Farrar, Straus and Giroux, LLC.

  My gratitude to the Hambidge Center for the Creative Arts and to Converse College, where, as the Sara Lura Mathews Self Writer in Residence in 2004, I was able to work on this manuscript.

  Thank you to George Ella Lyon, whose concluding poem in our renshi circle provided the final image for "Halloween Again."

  These poems owe much to Ann Munck and the late Arch Becklheimer, my writing teachers at Wesleyan College and cherished friends thereafter.

  I am grateful to Lynn Walterick for her friendship and for her help with preparing this manuscript.

For my daughter Corinna

Contents

PART 1

Again

We come back emptied,
to nourish and resist
the words of coming to rest:

birthplace, roofbeam, whitewash,
flagstone, hearth.

—SEAMUS HEANEY, "The Birthplace"

COASTAL PLAIN

The only clouds
forming are crow clouds,

the only shade, oaks
bound together in a tangle of oak

limbs that signal the wind
coming, if there is any wind

stroking the flat
fields, the flat

swatch of corn.
Far as anyone's eye can see, corn's

dying under the sky
that repeats itself either as sky

or as water
that won't remain water

for long on the highway: its shimmer
is merely the shimmer

of one more illusion that yields
to our crossing as we ourselves yield

to our lives, to the roots
of our landscape. Pull up the roots

and what do we see but the night
soil of dream, the night

soil of what we call
home. Home that calls

and calls
and calls.

AGAIN

I lie down in her sea bed that bears
me back home to the nothing left
after her house burned around it.

Her lavender handkerchief knotted
round nickels and dimes. On her dresser
a brooch in the shape of a peacock's tail.

Organdy curtains that breathed in
and out when she opened the windows
for March to blow through like a lioness

stalking the boxwoods or a lamb bleating
out by the pump house. Her hairpins
sown over the rugs. Her voluminous apron.

Her false teeth that grinned
every night from a tall iced-tea glass
as she pulled off her house dress,

her shimmy, her bloomers
that even now swell like a mainsail with
nothingness. Lorna Doone shortbread

she nibbled till she fell asleep, leaving crumbs
in the bed sheets like sand from the white beach
at Panama City whenever I crawled into bed

with her body that smelled of the ocean
at low tide and tasted of salt
when she pulled me too close to her.

SCUPPERNONGS

They ripened to myth on her tongue, sweetness
always beyond reach, out there at the edge
of abandoned farms, back in the thickets
where no decent woman dared go. Not that she
scorned the mayhaws her black neighbors left
at her door. Toiling hours in tropical swelter,
she boiled them down into a red syrup

salvaged in jelly jars. How much of her sweat
she stirred into that crimson stock I still
contemplate when it comes time to make jelly
again and I find myself roaming the fruit stalls
till I smell them, lifting both hands full,
as she would have done, to my nose,
understanding why she bent to every plum,

melon, and peach, every strip of fresh sugar cane.
Thus have these scuppernongs ripened
for too long inside my refrigerator.
Past time to ward off the coming rot,
time to remember how she'd set to work
with no recourse to Sure-Gel. Just lemon and
sugar. A spoon. Cheesecloth. Most of a morning

or afternoon, watching the syrup drip slowly,
then more slowly still down the spoon's sticky
edge. Leaving everything it touched, as always,
a mess, and for what? On my windowsill,
seven jars through which the light of this late
summer afternoon takes its time, quickening
each pot of pale amber juices to sweet everlasting.

HALLOWS

1.

These leaves at my window,
death-speckled black oak and blood-maple,

fall to the earth into which
she was sealed, leaving me

to imagine I see through the hollows
of what were her eyes how another day

breaks on the backs of the scrub pines
that stand up to welcome it.

2.

She was no saint.
She never fasted,
and if she prayed,
I never heard her

aside from the *Lawsy*
she uttered as down
she sank onto the dark
of the chamber pot
while I tried to be sleeping.

She stirred up the fire
to a roar every morning and beat
the dough smooth, shoved it into the oven
to bake and be eaten. When I hear Pavarotti
sing *Panis Angelicus,* I see her hands
deep in the dough bowl,

and I hear the fire in the stove rumble,
I hear her clucking and sighing,
she who could never on this earth
deliver unto any table a dry piece of cornbread,

whose old-fashioned cakes
that lay solid as flesh on the plates
put to shame every paper-thin
slice of the town-ladies' angelfood cakes.
(Any honest-to-god angel

would have preferred them,
a dollop of whipped cream atop
every thick slice and after that, oh,
just a touch of her Christmas divinity.)

3.
Los Muertos. The dead.
They are out there this morning,
in the woods with the busy squirrels
laying up treasures on earth,
this heaven of acorns and walnuts.
This granary.

These last dawns before the leaves go,
I wake early to watch from the window
my dead ones out there in the woods
leaf by leaf come
to rest on the ground
where at last they have nothing
to say beyond what's meant
to lie on the earth and be claimed by it.

COMING TO REST

1.

THE NAME

Because she'd not bury
the name with the dead child,
she made her surviving five children
swear they'd pass it on
to the first daughter born to them.

Another name for letting go.
Or holding on.

Another name for home.

2.

BIRTHDAY GHAZAL

Why this old Persian form for today, of all days?
Why not sonnet or blank verse to help me take hold?

Down to the wire goes the season's gold,
late this year, so long it took to take hold.

I don't care that my days tumble down
to the compost pile. I want to look, to take hold.

Seize the day. *Carpe diem,* if you like.
Bite down hard on the hook and take hold.

Down the creek float the leavings of what I once was.
Just a girl. Mostly waiting for luck to take hold.

Last night rain kept the roof busy scolding
me, *wake up you dumb cluck and take hold.*

I've already answered my e-mail, my voice
mail, my snail mail. My real work? To take hold.

Kathryn died too young. Age twelve. Now she tolls
in the dust of my name: to come back, to take hold.

3.
SINKING

The aunt I was named after died too young.
She sank at age twelve
into diabetic pneumonia. Then coma,

too pretty a word for her dying. Why cling
to another old form like this no-holds-
barred song for my aunt who died too young

to care about romance? What good is a song
now, to her? Or to me? Maybe I've grown too old
for such artifice, as if I'm trapped in a coma

of middle-aged dullness. My tongue
slips on names. But not hers. But why dwell
on her death? So she died, much too young,

not at all like an angel who could do no wrong,
not at all blonde & pretty as I had been told.
When she sank into that final coma,

she must have looked ugly. I can't make this
villanelle sing, no matter what I've been told
about Kathryn, who died too young,
years before insulin, of diabetic pneumonia.

4.
STUCK

She smooths her skirt and squints at me.
I don't know what to say. Or why she's come.
The clock's stopped ticking on the wall. Back home
again, she sees what I see, same old creek

reflecting nothing but a sky where trees
fish with their lines of moss all day. *Let's thumb
a ride to town,* she dares. *Let's make the phone lines hum
above these droughty fields. Now that I'm free*

I'm getting out of here. She says she wants to hear
the latest gossip, wants to have a little fun.
She tells me everything that hangs around
too long gets stuck. I nod. I don't dare
ask her why she's here, this dust I've stirred from
sleep. This shell of light. This sullen hologram.

5.
FREE

This nameless creek
almost obscured by shade
where she was last seen
by the camera lens
keeps rushing through me
as she hikes her skirt
and stands wanting to be
brave enough to walk
into the current,
sickly girl whose cropped
hair won't blow
in the summer
wind, *too short,*
too short, she cries,
coming to rest
in the photograph.

I LISTEN

to the old hymn
of April again,
dawn beginning the same
way my grandmother's jewelry box
opens, its little tune tinkling
as the ballerina turns

and my mother
sits down at her vanity,
mulling which silver
chain hooked
round her neck
or her wrist,
which distillation
of light from her earlobes.
The day burns like fire
at her fingertips,

rousing the birds
to a reveille
my daughter conducts
from her bassinet,
wide awake now
while I lie in bed wanting
the words to this music,
as if I'm a Sunday school child

again watching the choir
sing its loud hallelujahs
while, dumb as a stone,
I sat waiting for Jesus
to touch every ear,
every tongue
of his mute children,
whispering,
Eph-pha-tha.
Be opened!

PNEUMONIA

And then the dark fell and "there has never"
I said, "been a poem to an antibiotic:
never a word to compare with the odes on
the flower of the raw sloe for fever"
—EAVAN BOLAND, "The Journey"

All Sunday night I rocked her,
stunned by fear and wondering
how women once got through
such nights without a doctor near,

no balm but cherry bark or boneset
steeped to bitter tea, or mustard
laced with lard and cornmeal
laid upon a poultice sheet.

By morning she was limp.
At 6:00 AM her fever hit a hundred five,
her breathing like a wounded kitten's
after being broken by a heavy boot.

We lowered her into a tub of lukewarm water
while she whimpered, then grew quieter
as the ibuprofen took effect. I called
the doctor who for days had told me *wait.*

Again he said it. So we waited
till his office opened, but by then
she was too weak to walk.
Her father carried her inside. We sat

while someone called Admissions
and the doctor told us all was set
for her, a private room, an x-ray,
intravenous penicillin, she'd be fine,

no need to worry. Glazed eyes,
that's what I remember: nothing there.
We watched her taken into x-ray,
then watched lab-technicians try

and try again to stick a vein.
Then watched two nurses hook her up
to spools of tubes and drips.
Sat down and watched her. Watched

her. Nurses came and went. Or didn't
come. One bleached blonde read
her numbers wrong, no fever
she announced, though I could see it

burning in her eyes, her breath,
so when the retching started, I rang
non-stop. It took them 40 minutes
to come back. I bit my lip. And sat

again. At last she slept, her breathing
slowed, and when the doctor came
at dusk, he said *Her fever's broken.*
X-ray's fine. This time tomorrow,

she'll go home. But I kept watch all night;
between the nurses' checks,
I lay beside her on a cot and listened
to her breathing, touched her skin,

now cool, as slowly down
the i.v. tube into the needle rooted
in her vein, the saving liquid dripped
and dripped until the daylight came.

HALLOWEEN

for Cory, who chose the magic words

A princess, she likes the way silk
sounds, how smooth on her rose-
colored tongue, yet thrilling as copper
coins flipped. Heads or tails. Lost
or found. Daughter, daughter, the pumpkin
grins under the full moon, the hem

of your dress sweeps the hem
of the black curtain falling like silk
over everything, changing the pumpkin
you carved to look fierce to a lost
clown who sits on the sidewalk and begs for a copper
coin, too scared to tell how he rose

from the dead, wearing one perfect rose
in his buttonhole, no longer pumpkin
but suave as the sibilance silk
makes, a gentleman tossing a copper
coin into a beggar's cup, wafting cologne from the hem
of his handkerchief. Everyone knows it's a lost

art, our show of pretending we've lost
nothing lasting to time, as if copper
coins aren't squandered, as if a little girl's silk
dress will never go back to its rose-
wood and mothballs a muddy mess, hems
falling down. If I asked him, the pumpkin

would say he knows nothing of this. Let us pumpkins
be pumpkins, he'd say. Let all little girls lost
in their masquerade be found alive by a copper
who talks tough but scrubs muddy hems
for a princess who cries. Let him pocket her rose-
colored glasses and carry her home. "Silk,"

she whispers, but she wants to say something silk
only means the beginning of. Ask any pumpkin
what happens next. Princess grows up and has lost
all the petals she saved from her ring-around-rose
garden. Time's trick. Its treat? Kiss the hem
of her skirt: how it carries the faint taste of copper,

the fragrance of rose-water! Under the copper
moon, she lifts the hem of her silk skirt and bows to the pumpkin,
a real princess lost in the moment, her brief kingdom.

EMPTY

So tender, I said, "Remember this.
It will be good for you to retrace this path

when you have grown away and stand at last
at the very centre of the empty city."
—SEAMUS HEANEY, "Changes"

Crossing the Skyway bridge
for the first time, I see what she's chosen,
alabaster city floating clear of my clinging
as station by toll station, we drop our coins into baskets,
a half dozen lanes running over with cars.

I forget to look over the railing at lake water,
bright sails, I forget everything but my mother,
before the train left for New York, pinning even more money
inside my bra, warning: "Don't wander too far
from the group. Don't get caught in the subway doors,
don't stand too close to the tracks. Always deadbolt
the hotel door." That was the last year our school
sent its Seniors to New York. *It's nothing but jungle now*
I hear my father say. *Wouldn't want one of mine living there.*

This is Chicago, I tell him. Not New York.
And isn't your grandson now living in Brooklyn? My father shrugs,
settles back into the hum of my own questions.
Where will she live and how far from the campus? How many
armed robberies this year? And traffic,
how will she cross streets without
being run down? "Lock your doors," I say
as we exit the Skyway. She laughs at me.

Let her. I can't let her go without leaving my
mother's fears with her, they're all I can muster right now.
We will climb in our empty car soon enough
and drive home without her. So let us unload books

and clothing, her numerous boxes of earrings,
my bundles of medicines she shrugs aside
when I warn her she'll need them come bitter
times. Icy stairs. Frigid streets she'll walk
without my knowing where. This is her city now,
let her stand at the heart of it, hearing its
sirens, arterial rumblings of El trains
and buses. Its welcoming emptiness.

NOBODY'S BABY TONIGHT

A blues paradelle

The trucks on Interstate 65 go thundering by.
The trucks on Interstate 65 go thundering by.
Now, one by one, the lights in the sky turn into planes.
Now, one by one, the lights in the sky turn into planes.
Thundering, the planes turn into trucks on Interstate 65.
Now the lights one by one in the sky go by.

Tonight our car is heavy with our daughter's belongings.
Tonight our car is heavy with our daughter's belongings.
We are driving her back to Chicago.
We are driving her back to Chicago.
Tonight Chicago is driving our car, our daughter.
Heavy with belonging we are, backs to her.

How many more times will I have to say goodbye?
How many more times will I have to say goodbye?
Nobody's talking. Not even the radio.
Nobody's talking. Not even the radio.
How many radios talking to nobodies? (Even
more goodbyes?) I will not have the time to say

"Go back" to planes, trucks, cars thundering into lights.
Heavy with belonging, not even our daughter is
talking. By and by in Chicago, I will have to say more
goodbyes. How many? One to her, one to the sky.
Now time is driving Interstate 65.
Turn on the radio! Let's be nobody's tonight.

STILL TO US AT TWILIGHT

Beauty without the beloved
is a spear through the heart.
I hear that on t.v. just hours after leaving her

outside the dormitory gate, watched over by gargoyles,
in suburban Chicago. My husband and I drinking whiskey
in our motel room watch American Movie Classics

till he falls asleep. The same day we carried her home
from the hospital, her grandmother said, *You will be*
so afraid sometimes, you will not be able to close

your eyes. Sometimes? I can make myself scared every day
if I want to. Other days I don't have to,
the world does it for me. That's when I lie awake·

tasting blood after slicing my tongue on the cake knife
when I was a child sneaking sweets from the kitchen.
Why do I find the word *love* so hard to speak?

Say it, *love,* and my tongue bleeds. My heart
flops like a catfish before the knife guts it.
This time tomorrow, I'll be 3 states away from her,

one time zone ahead of her. (The ways we keep missing
each other, and time at the heart of it all!) But look,
that incendiary sunset over the black Indiana plains

makes me reach for my husband. My heart at the sight
of him surges. But he's asleep. Almost snoring and what now,
another old war movie? The field doctor holding his knife

to an open flame. I turn my eyes away. Cut off
the t.v. and try to sleep. Blood on a knife. On my tongue.
The taste of beauty all night in my mouth.

CHICAGO BOUND

Your twenty-first birthday,
so we arrive early at the airport,
plenty of time before take-off,
the rain steady, ugly gray
sky while the radio cheers us

on, Jimmy Rogers and *Sweet Home
Chicago,* just what we need on
this Friday you turn twenty-one.
Come on, come on, let's get a move on.
I'm ready, Daddy, to leave this town.

I hold my breath while the plane rises,
muddy clouds all the way up
till we come out the other side into
the stratosphere, lapis lazuli and white
shag carpet all the way there.

Nobody at home up here. Makes me
feel lonesome till I see the beverage cart
rolling toward us and lower my tray.
What's for lunch? Nothing much.
Cookie, sandwich, a small Baby Ruth.

Captain's voice from the cockpit
keeps telling us how long before
we'll come down. Soon it's time for a snooze
while this plane flies us over the heartland
to you in your Shakespeare class,

old boss man Lear raving blank verse,
still crazy after all these years. Just a little while
longer, we'll be on the ground
where we'll hop a train south to the campus,
a place I like better than this flimsy

carpet of clouds on which I cannot walk
to you. I need green fields
to do that, some tough city blocks,
Kimbark, Ellis, East Hyde Park.
Give me boulevard, avenue,

chemin, rue, strasse, calle,
avenida, el camino, whatever
you want to call it, Baby, if it's down
there on earth where you are,
it's Sweet Home. I'll take it.

PART 2

Singing to Salt Woman

In memory of Alice Mathews

When people come for her salt,
they must stand before her and say,
"Grandmother, give me some water."
—"Shooting Chant"

A-MA'*

*What do you want,
I asked as you lay
on the hospital bed.*

*Water,
you said.
I want water.*

*So I filled a glass,
held it steady
while you drank,*

*remembering
that those setting forth
on a journey*

*must drink from
the wellsprings of home
before leaving.*

Water in Cherokee

TAKING LEAVE

Now that our camping gear's packed
on the floor of the truck,
I hear birds swooping lower
than usual this morning
sing *stay home.*
The river has suddenly come back,
for days I'd forgotten it lived here beneath us,
and I can see Indian paintbrushes flicking
their tongues from the shadows.

What is it about leaving
that makes what we're leaving reach out to us,
beg to be noticed?

Why, when I'm ready to leave
must I always turn back?

Take one last
look around.

DREAMING THROUGH TENNESSEE

Halfway to Nashville, I'm drifting
off into a landscape of light
taking shape on a lone butte

or mesa, an oxbow
of rock being worn down
to rubble and hastened away

on the flash-floods that glut
the arroyos. My eyes close.
The South, running rampant

with kudzu, can wait
till I wake up to show me
the same makeshift signs

that I've seen all my life
threaten God's coming back.
I'm dreaming God's gone

for good to inhabit
the desert like wind
or like silence at noonday

when nothing dares
move from its small peace
of merciful shadow.

CUMBERLAND GAP

More than 400 years after
the natives who named
their way over these mountains

have disappeared,
leaving what used to be frontier
for us to call *home*

with its family names
given rivers and summits,
a few native words

left behind to lure
tourists to motels
and souvenir shops,

what's native now?
I cast a fearful glance into the dark
before we bank our fire and crawl

into our sleeping bags. All night
the woods sound a nativeness
few of us dare let ourselves go

into. What would we find
there? Nothing we'd know
how to know.

BLACK ROAD

that blisters through
hardscrabble
westward to what lies
beyond what we think
we see, how many
miles across
drought-stubbled flats
must we drive,
every word baked
away but the one
that means water
no matter whose
language: *eau, agua,*
pah, nahe, a-ma'?
A city of grain
elevators and storage bins
shimmers ahead in the distance.
How many miles
we try to guess. Ten?
Or twenty-five?
Oil derricks stand around,
giving us no answer,
nor do the small houses
looking as if only dust devils
live there with no love
for anything human a long way
from home. *Misère*
the mourning doves croon
in the empty fields. Sunday
in west Oklahoma, the sermon
of here and now: Life
is an endless drive over
the panhandle. God is a King

Snake of asphalt whose
every commandment is
follow me
follow me
follow me.

DEAD END IN PUEBLO, COLORADO

Parked on a nameless back street
while we wait out a thunderstorm
churning the sidewalks to muddy

arroyos, I try to write postcards.
I shuffle my pack till I find
the right scene, distant Sangre

de Cristos no more than a backdrop
to one of those white crosses
wreathed in a garland of red plastic

flowers that's placed by the roadside
to signify death happened
here. Dearest Alice, I write,

what's it like where you are?
Always high noon,
or midnight? Or else afternoon

with its sodden eternity
heavy as tent-canvas over you?
Tell me the truth, if you wanted

to howl with the ghost of some
long-extinct wolf, would He let you?
And if not, would you do it anyway?

Alice, I fear where you are
must be damp and cold. Cramped.
And silent as any dead wolf's throat.

CONTEMPLATION

For this the monks journeyed
to Mont-Saint-Michel, the French guide explained
as we gathered round high windows
over the sea that looked dead as the past
from that distance, yet never stopped sounding,
becoming in that moldy vestibule God's voice
insisting beyond what his monks sang of faith
to the edge of all singing,
to silence.

The silence
of endless sand shimmers at noon
like an ocean becalmed
as we journey toward Zion like pilgrims
determined to pass through the wilderness
unscathed by doubt. We see no other
car on this back road in Utah,
the scenic route south through the hoo-doos
of San Rafael.

Each sandstone formation arises
like Mont-Saint-Michel itself, refuge to creatures
with no other place they can go to be saved,
for we know in the Christian re-vision of this land
they have no immortal souls. Cast not at all
in our Lord's image but in the image
of Serpent, they coil in a fissure of rock,
where they contemplate sunlight and shade,
left behind by a god who once sang in the swell
of an ocean gone six million years
from this continent.

ZUNI

A few miles from town,
so the legend goes, Salt Woman
sleeps in her lake bed

and only the words that are native
to each place can waken her,
asking for water again

and again in the earth's many
tongues. Maybe *native* means nothing
if not our own way of recovering,

back to the first wind
that quickened it, what we call
home. Like a worm hole

that memory leaps through
as if time had no meaning,
which to the spirits of place

(not to mention the physicists
juggling their data) it hasn't.
But right now the noon sun

beats down on the main street
of Zuni. The lunch traffic stalls,
tourists wander the craft shops

while outside town, Salt woman
sleeps on her lake bottom,
waiting to be summoned

into the season's rush,
native and non-native milling
about in the wake

of a creation story
whose ripples keep spreading
beyond comprehension.

CONTINENTAL DIVIDE

Too soon the waters will flow east
with our leaving. These mesas cannot last
much longer. Tomorrow they'll flatten
out into the high plains of Texas.

Somewhere to the south of us, Acoma
floats in the clouds, out of reach, like a vision
of pure gold that blazed nearly four hundred years
ago, blinding the eyes of the Conquistadors.

For two hours I shopped the turquoise
and silver of Zuni,
believing in signs hammered into a shape
I could carry home. Nothing but trays

full of trinkets reduced to their sale prices,
fifteen percent
off of all stock, the squash blossoms,
conchas, and Hopi rings waiting

for tourists to handle them,
asking, "So what does this mean,
this design?" And the sales girl responding, "No
meaning. Just something they dreamed up."

In piles by the door, slabs
of turquoise lay, nobody's merchandise yet,
only something the earth had made, color of deep
water borne neither east nor west.

EDGE OF PLAINS

On this, the first morning of going
home, I cannot face east,
so ride looking back at the last mesa
left before panhandle, swearing my fealty
to rock I have clung to
as I climbed the last inches up
to the canyon rim, chanting
the ages of sandstone for grit:
Moenkopi
and Navajo,
Chinle,
Kayenta,
their layers of mud

sculpted into the structures
of *I-oo-goone,* later named
Mukuntaweap by the one-fisted Powell.
We know it as Zion,
so christened by Mormons
who searched for a heavenly paradise,
seeing its landforms as altars
and courts of the only true God.

To the dead Anasazi
who left us no name to decipher,
this cul-de-sac canyon meant earthly
repose on its bedrock of shale.
There a man might dream
visions of huntsman and hunted
to carve on its cliff walls come light,
while around him the canyon wind keened
like the earth herself
chanting her way back through time
to the dawn of the first morning.

TENT DREAM

Bring your knife and your coloring book,
an old woman's voice said,

so I tried to follow. I knew
day was waiting downriver. I heard

many voices advise me along the way,
mumbling in ancient Apache

or old-country Gaelic, a shudder
of Gullah tongues parting the salt

water. Native or non-native,
sometimes we hear the same voices,

like Zuni corn chanting
my grandmother up from the dust

into one last day walking her bean-rows
and suddenly so much green

singing around me, I take out my knife
and cut through to daylight.

ALMOST HOME

As the Blue Ridge begins
to take shape, its backbone
of oldest rock greener
than I believed possible last week
in Utah, a silent rain
seeps into corn and tobacco
roots, Queen Anne's Lace blooming
from ditches. These low places
hold water longest, their puddles
of frog spawn that promise
the patient sublunary legs
of a Keatsian pond singer multiplied
ten thousand fold.
When I roll down the car window,
I hear their fierce territorial chant
and remember the young soldier
sitting beside me, whispering
into the window glass,
Home
Home,
as our bus arrived late in another
small town where nobody
stood waiting to meet him.

STOPPING

the car, we at first notice only the silence,
nobody to welcome us home but the jiggety-jig
of these bugs in the glow of our headlights.
The trees stand around as if waiting

for us to acknowledge their presence.
Our garden's run wild and the blackberry bushes
do battle for every last inch of what used to be
backyard. When hoot owls

begin to call down from the summit
of Buzzard's Roost, I feel
my skin answer. Home again,
precious little to show

for my journey, I'm ready to say let
the crickets begin! Let me stand
in the darkness a little while listening
before I walk into my empty house.

A'MA*

First thing I do
when I walk in, I reach
for the salt on my table

and say to the devil
behind me, Here's salt
in your eyes. Take this

winding sheet
you want to wrap me in,
what is it now

but a tablecloth
after my grandmother's own
heart, a flutter of white

linen settling, its wing-
span the measure of all things
I see spread before me.

*Salt in Cherokee

This should always be done,
a song at the beginning
and the end
of the journey,
and so for you, Alice,
I stand in my kitchen
and sing of
the way you held each
of the raspberries
I brought you
up to the light before
placing them into your mouth,
one by one,
until they were gone.

PART 3
Closer

But there is still the melody, the full
and unmistakable fluency, the call
and response of memory—
first skin, then breath,
then the rich embrace of what's left.
—HEATHER ROSS MILLER, "Gypsy with Baby"

THE STILL HERE AND NOW

for Ruth

Wesleyan College, 11/6/04

This fragrance I've never been able to name,
floating past on the skin of an eighteen year old,
still invites me to stand on the loggia again,
afternoon ticking down into dark,
asking *What am I doing here?*
lost among strangers with hair more
bouffant than mine, clothing more stylish.

Soon I'd learn the words for what I couldn't find
in my closet: Bass weejuns, madras, and Villager.
As for the name of that scent mingling
now with aroma of barbecue served on the porch,
it would have to be French, I imagined,
Ma Griffe, L'air du Temps, Insouciance,
not my mother's stale *Emeraude* clinging to me
from our goodbye embraces. Now dusk would be
shrouding my father's farm, doves mourning
out in the empty fields. I knew my way back
to all that. Don't think for a moment I didn't

wish I had the courage to set out for home.
But just then the sun set. The lamps bloomed
like storybook tulips. The campus unfolded
around me its labyrinth that like a medieval pilgrim
I'd walk until I reached the center where I'd find
no Rose Window as I saw later at Chartres
sifting light down upon us, but tall classroom windows
that shook when the Rivoli train passed. I still walk
those pathways at night, dreaming arias spiraling
forth from the practice rooms, each dorm a beehive
of desk lamps and phones ringing endlessly.

Time, say some physicists, does not exist.
Sheer Illusion. Each moment a still frame,
as though in a movie reel unspooling out to the edge
of the universe. Each now forever.
So let my first afternoon darken to first night.
Inside a small room overlooking a golf course
and woodland, a small bed waits,
heaped with my unpacked belongings.
I slowly walk toward it, my nostrils still seeking
a fragrance I now name *Siempre* because
the next day I sit down to learn Spanish,
not French. In my best cursive
I write my name on each blank sheet I'm given.
The ginkgo trees flutter their luminous handkerchiefs:
Buenos Días, Bonjour, Willkommen.

Again and again I come back
to the start of this journey. I stand looking down
at the fountain, as if to say *Here I am.*
There you are, water sings to our gathering voices.
The loggia is filling with girls wanting supper,
and now she whose fragrance awakened my senses
so many years back brushes by and the wake
of her passage still trembles around me.

THE EXOTICS

for Robert Watson

The exotics, as the witty department head called us,
we gathered each Thursday, if I can remember it right
after thirty-two years, in the seminar room
of the library, eager for what Bob would say
as he scrutinized, word by word,
what we had brought him. We passed our new poems
round the table and waited to read aloud,
palms sweaty, tongues dry from suddenly doubting
that anything inside the dark of our voices could sing
worth Bob's listening. Bertha's brave circus beasts
galloped in sawdust. Then Ellen's glass kept harping back
to the same jangle. I heard my cornfields beginning
to sprout a shy whisper. And Rick's *Soledades: O Luminous
Afternoon,* when with the fanfare of hyacinths, Pat levitated
her dead grandpa's flimsy fedora! The odor of hyacinths
that April I'm not ashamed to say followed me
everywhere, promising more poems than I believed
possible. Poetry or prose, we debated,
and let pass our judgment till some other time
when the question seemed less dull. We'd engineer fire-
works, our poems bursting forth in a plumage
of red smoke. But once when I stubbed my True
cigarette into the trash can and rough drafts of poems
began smoldering, George muttered, "Jesus
H. Christ," and ran out with a Styrofoam cup
to fetch water. So Joel extinguished the first nip
of flame with his breath and swore he would write
poems that burned clean through the page,
as if nobody knew he was falling in love with the air
itself teasing him into her circles
within circles till he was so dizzy
he could see stars in the smallest reflection
of night in his black Chevy's rear mirror.

That April, King was gunned down
and the city shut tight in its curfew at sunset,
we walked every afternoon roundabout Spring Garden,
looking for poems we could bring back to Bob,
not those blowsy pink dogwoods
that littered the campus with tickets to easy romance,
but the hard freight that rattled our teeth
till we wanted to shout at the crazy caboose-man who waved
as he disappeared into the junkyards
at city's end: Take Me!
O Central of Georgia, where are you tonight?
Do your boxcars still wait at the corner of Highland
and shudder with wanting to keep their long lines moving
on into margins I can't see the limits of?
I confess I have gone nowhere.
I'm still caught inside the same lines I've been trying
to write since we walked to Bob's class
in a wind I am sure I remember
demanding so fiercely we hold our poems close to our bodies
as if out of fear
(or desire)
they would blow away into a jungle
of burning wings
green tongues
and we would have no other choice but to follow.

NETS

for Dennis Zaborowski

1.

That the movement of railroad tracks
through an industrial landscape could be,
as you like to say, sinuous,
never occurred to me, raised as I was
in a landscape where sinuous means how a fence makes
its way around fields, how the telephone wires
hang like curtain swag over the distance.
And yet, in these paintings
you show us, I can see tracks winding
almost like fences past freight yard and warehouses.
They draw the gray scene of Cleveland
together as surely as your charcoal lines cast
a wide net to catch in their tangled
connections the father whose back is a bridge
for his children, the mother who waits
in her bed after childbirth, her heavy breasts
filling with milk while her eyes close.
Beyond her the turning of wheels never ceases.

2.

The source of our art is what we see
outside our first window: Your Cleveland,
for instance, its monochromatic web riddled
with churches, among them
the spires of Saint Stanislaus rising
against the industrial wilderness,
icons of blood and transcendence still gleaming
way back in your memory,
although by now you have found your own
icons: those slats of corroded tin,
paint peeling down to the good shade of rust

you like. Color of earth itself,
first pigment smeared on the underground
walls of the Paleolithic.

3.
To reach the Great Hunt of Lascaux,
you must crawl through a network of tunnels
so narrow you writhe on your belly
as if you're a snake, till the way opens suddenly
onto a vast chamber, line upon line
on its walls re-creating the beasts of the Ice Age,
their teeming herds vanishing into the dark
corners. You raise your lantern
and see on a rocky apse that fierce shamanic
form: black-painted sorcerer, He
whom you know as the Artist: yourself
at the moment you see takin:g shape on the paper
before you the face of a man
in a crowded bar somewhere in Cleveland, Ohio.

4.
Line
for the caveman worked
magic when he made it give
shape to bison
and mammoth. For you
is it anything less

than a mystery
out of which you summon
figures held fast
in their stories of human
entanglement? That

little girl looking
into her mother's face, what is she
thinking? That man
leaning back as if he could
escape from his lover's
embrace?

STILL LIFE

Or *Stilleben,* as my German great-grandmother
might have described it, if she'd not forgotten the old words
of childhood. The only one she ever painted,

it sits with the rest of the junk in our attic,
a total disaster, its dull globs of pigment
heaped into a crude wooden bowl.

Each grape,
every apple sucked dry of all substance,
like words that no longer contain any meaning.

She must have stepped back
from the canvas and promised herself
no more domestic interiors:

this apple,
this platter,
this life,

and none other. To paint
her way out
of the commonplace,

she turned to ships
being tossed upon silver-gray churnings,
the tumble of surf

over bare feet of girls dragging
fishing-nets, Indians paddling canoes
down the rapids of

some Northwest Passage,
the moon always full
and a cloud always scudding

across it. In each of her best paintings,
she followed water,
and not what the women call here

in the mountains she later would live
among, *dead*
water, lying in basins

all night by the sick bed
or turning to slime in a pig trough.
The water she wanted

can't wait
to jump creekbed
or sandbags stacked sky-high

to get where it's going.
Has water but one life?
she wrote in her journal

the morning her train
left the Black Hills for points
south and southeast.

Have I?

SELF-PORTRAIT WITH SHADES

No Frida Kahlo, I find myself
bored by my face in the mirror.
No parrot to perch on my shoulder,
no Tehuana rebozo,
no Aztecan baubles
distending my earlobes.
No man I love so much I'd brand
his diminutive face into my forehead.

My own native dress from the provinces?
A feedsack smock spattered with bacon grease,
lap smeared with blood
from a white-leghorn, neck lately wrung.

I pick up my charcoal and glare
at the bathroom glass.
Die Alte Marschallin
sitting alone at her vanity.
Frown and she frowns.
Wink and she winks, launching into
"La Vie en Rose," her best imitation of Piaf,
no rose-colored glasses,
just cut-rate and horn-
rimmed from Wal-Mart.

My pencil snakes over the paper,
then stalls for an instant,
before digging in,
executing wild spirals, it zig-zags itself into
corners. Then stops.
I look down. My eyes too large,
unblinking and blind. My mouth sealed
by cross-hatching. My rootwad of hair
looks about to sprout serpents

above shadow caving my cheek,
my chin like an axehead cleaving the page.
I once saw the same sweep of bone jutting
forth out of blue satin, yes,
there she was, kinswomen urging me closer
and closer as I tried,
but not hard enough, not to see
as I let myself be lifted over her casket.

LOS MUERTOS

Tonight my long dead from the flatlands
come back again, climbing the hill
with their stories. That old woman lifting
the bacon slabs into a skillet
and licking her fingers, she smells
like a thousand cold suppers laid out
on her burned table. Just one more
mouthful, she wheedles,
insisting I sample the pork skins

my uncle loved so much he'd eat till
his stripe-shirted belly swelled.
Belching and farting his way
to his pickup truck, he wipes his hands
on his backside as if he had never been taught

any manners, forthright as his daddy
who bangs on my door every November.
He has walked three hundred miles
from the homeplace to tell me these leaves
need some raking, that fire needs
some fat-wood to make it jump,
keep him warm,

all of them wanting the same thing,
a warm house, tonight,
even Kathryn, who dares me
to let her in so she can stomp
through my rooms, slamming doors
like the spoiled girl she was,
her desire for what she heard
her mama sing over and over,
the mocking bird Daddy would bring
from the store where he worked as
a bagboy on Saturdays,

cut short
while she languished,
sullen on pallets beside the fire,
watching the youngest play pick-up sticks,
hating his health that would last
only three years before he too lost
weight and fell dead away into the trough
as he emptied the hog slops,
last thing he heard before fieldhands
came running, the doves
in the cornfields like destiny

which has the mournfulest
sound to it. I hear it shuffling through
oak leaves I should have raked yesterday.
It comes to call in a grease-spattered housedress
or dung-crusted workboots,
and sometimes it sits on my doorstep
and cries
like the young girl for whom
I was named,
who still haunts me
this night of all souls waking up again,
begging that she stay
alive for as long as I'll let her.

PRECIOUS LITTLE

The passageway down which they had
just gone was bright as the eye of a needle.
—EUDORA WELTY, *Losing Battles*

So we'd gathered to talk about writing,
remembering great ones who'd recently gone
from our midst and the various ways
they had followed each voice through

the needle's eye into the clearing of art,
when a novelist slouched
on the front row opined
that the only real subject is battle

and how men survive it.
I seethed while my student poets,
all of them women, sat waiting for someone
to challenge his vision of literature,

belligerent canon
where warring tribes battle it out
in their epics and blood-spattered novels.
"Miss Welty," I countered, "stayed

clear of the battlefield, if you recall.
She sat down every day at the same desk
and made language raise the world up
from the grave of our common amnesia."

He barely acknowledged
my comment. He wanted to flirt
with my students. He shrugged at me,
stood up and showed off the fit

of his tight jeans. My god,
what a chasm he opened up right there
between us: we stared like combatants
across the trench, loading our weapons,

his now on full frontal display,
along with a first novel already lobbed
to reviewers by Random House. As for me,
middle-aged poet, what were mine?

Precious little. The shot I recalled
having seen months ago of a woman my age
holding up to the camera a photo of daughter
or sister or good friend who'd disappeared

into the rubble of felled towers, the same woman
I had seen sifting through ruins in Fallujah
and Kabul, even now cringing
when she hears the gunfire in Baghdad,

a woman who stares back at me
when I'm dusting my daughter's face
framed on the shelf,
smiling out at a day that's been gone

for so long I can barely remember it,
nothing much going on, no bombs,
no fireworks, just late summer afternoon
and the dogs asleep under the oak tree.

HER DAETER

HER DAUGHTER

Charred dove nightingale still burning
—MIRZA GHALIB,

Baghdad, April 8, 2003

Four years younger than mine,
her daughter lies under the rubble.

She stands at the edge of it,
watching the men lifting one stone,

another, till out of the crater
they gently lift somebody's

body, a body she now
sees is female. She tries to recall

what her daughter was wearing,
but no scrap of clothing remains

on it. Whose body is it? She sees
no face. She sees no head.

At the edge of the crater she stands
while they swaddle the body in blankets

a neighbor has brought. Through
the blasted streets she calls

a name that gets lost
in the rattle of gunfire, a name

no one hears as they pull
from the rubble her daughter's

head, hair twisted round like
a rootwad, not blonde

like my daughter's, not waking
up as my daughter will be, being safe

on this morning in Texas, beginning
to brush her hair after her shower,

her face in the mirror as perfect as
always I see it, the fair skin

she wishes had South Asian
dusk in it, not Southern

sun from the fields of her mother's
line, as she examines

the scar on her temple,
the chin she believes looks

not quite smooth
enough, while her fingers

scroll over its surface
as if they are translating

Urdu, word after
unsteady word of a ghazal

that she must recite
today, all the while fearing

her voice will fail
even as she tries

to fill up the silence
with Ghalib's desire

to see, lost in the blaze
of the mirror

that holds her,
the face of the Beloved.

HALLOWEEN AGAIN

and time slides like silk
against silk.
Easy to get lost
in letting go
this time of year.
Lost letters.
Lost memories.
Lost copper
earrings a friend
gave me.
Split Silk,
I haven't forgotten
the name
of that church
on the far side
of home,
how it rose
from the roadside,
a hymn to the landscape
I passed through
where pumpkins
lay stacked beside fields
like the kindling
my ancestors gathered
for bonfires
on All Hallows Eve
when the veil
between seen
and unseen trembles
sheer as silk
through which
we might, if
we come close
enough, see
the other side
waiting for us

as a mirror waits
to be filled
with the bright
face of forever.

CLOSER

old road dreaming me back home
through coastal plain into the Gulf

stunted pines along the roadside
dripping with dark into night puddles

arcade of pecan trees into infinity
through which my memory roams

like spider webs over wounds
these bare branches over my eyes

maybe souls do flow into and out of the world—
that crow over corn stubble, scythe of light

off the truck's chrome, swish of an icy
mare's tail over the December sky

NOTES

SECTION EPIGRAPHS:

PART 1: Seamus Heaney, "The Birthplace," in *Station Island* (New York: Farrar, Straus and Giroux, 1985).

PART 2: "Shooting Chant," in *Changing Woman and Her Sisters,* Sheila Moon (San Francisco: Guild for Psychological Studies Publishing House, 1984).

PART 3: Heather Ross Miller, "Gypsy with Baby," in *Gypsy with Baby* (Hammond, LA: Louisiana Literature Press, 2005).

In "I Listen," the lines *"Eph-pha-tha. / Be opened!"* are from Mark 7:34.

"The Still Here and Now" was written for the inauguration of Ruth Austin Knox as twenty-fourth president of Wesleyan College in Macon, Georgia.

I am grateful for the essay "The Ghazal Itself: Translating Ghalib," by C. M. Naim (*Yale Journal of Criticism* 5, no. 1 [1992]) in which I discovered the W. S. Merwin translation used in "Her Daughter."